Desolation Wilderness
Fishing Guide

Jerome Yesavage

PORTLAND

The cover: *Entering the Desolation Wilderness from the Fallen Leaf Lake area on the trail to Triangle Lake.*

Copyright 1994 by Jerome Yesavage
ALL RIGHTS RESERVED. No part of this book may be reproduced without the written consent of the publisher, except in the case of brief excerpts in critical reviews and articles.
Published in 1994 by Frank Amato Publications
P.O. Box 82112, Portland, Oregon 97282
ISBN: 1-878175-62-9
UPC: 0-66066-00154-2
Book Design: Charlie Clifford
Printed in U.S.A.
10 9 8 7 6 5 4 3 2 1

Contents

Abstract 5
Dedication 5
Introduction 5
History 6

The Species 6
    Brook Trout 7   Browns 8
    Rainbows 7   Miscellaneous 8
    Goldens 7

Strategy 8
    Which Lakes to Fish 8   Reading a Lake 10
    When to Fish the Lakes 9   Float Tubes 11

Tactics and Tackle 12
    Spin Fishing 12   Fly Fishing 13

Wilderness Permits and Ethics 15
    Wilderness Regulations and
        Wilderness Ethics 15
    Fishing Ethics 17

Desolation Wilderness Section Map 19

Section 1: Echo Lakes 20
    Cup Lake 20   Tamarack Lake 22
    Saucer Lake 21   Ralston Lake 23
    Triangle Lake 21   Cagwin Lake 23
    Lost Lake 22

Section 2: Desolation Valley 24
    Avalanche Lake 24   Frata Lake 26
    Pitt Lake 25   Lake Aloha 26
    Ropi, Toem, Osma & Gefo Lakes..25   Lake Lucille & Lake Margery 27
    Pyramid and Waca Lakes 25   Lake Le Conte 27
    Desolation, Chain, Channel &
        American Lakes 25   Jabu Lake 27
    Lake Of The Woods 26

Section 3: Wright's Lake 28
   Lyon's Lake 28
   Lake Sylvia 28
   Grouse Lake........................28
   Hemlock Lake 29
   Smith Lake 29
   Twin Lake...........................29
   Island Lakes 29
   Tyler Lake 29
   Gertrude Lake 30
   Maud Lake 30
   Barrett Lake 30
   Lawrence Lake 30
   Top Lake 30
   Lake Number 5 31

Section 4: Rockbound Valley 32
   Rockbound Lake 32
   Rubicon Reservoir..............32
   Clyde Lake 32
   Lake Doris 33
   Lake Lois 33
   Lake Schmidell 33
   Leland Lakes 33
   Zitella, Horseshoe & the 4-Q's Lakes.34
   Highland Lake 34

Section 5: Meeks Creek..35
   Lake Genevieve..................35
   Crag Lake 35
   Hidden Lake 35
   Shadow Lake 36
   Stony Ridge Lake 36
   Cliff Lake............................37
   Rubican Lake......................37
   Grouse Lakes......................37
   Phipps Lake 38

Section 6: Eagle Creek 39
   Eagle Lake..........................39
   Lower Velma Lake..............39
   Middle Velma Lake............40
   Upper Velma & Fontanillis Lake ..40
   Dick's Lake 40
   Granite Lake 40
   Azure Lake 41
   Snow Lake..........................41
   Tallac & Kalmia Lakes 42

Section 7: Fallen Leaf Lake..43
   Floating Island Lake 43
   Cathedral Lake 43
   Heather Lake 43
   Susie Lake 44
   Half Moon Lake 44
   Gilmore Lake 45
   Grass Lake..........................45

Further Reading..46

Guide to Fishing the Desolation Wilderness

Abstract

The Desolation Wilderness is a 100-square-mile federal "wilderness area" directly to the west of Lake Tahoe in California. The granite and glaciers of the Sierra Nevada have blessed this region by leading to the formation of over 100 lakes of all sizes. This guide presents seven sections of the Desolation. Specific information is included about access to its lakes, the type of fish in each, where fish may be found in the lake and important clues about angling tactics and strategy.

Proceeds from this guide will be used to fund biological studies in the Wilderness.

The author started trout fishing over 30 years ago in the eastern United States. He has spent many years engaged in technical rock climbing in Yosemite and the back country Sierra Nevada. Over the last 20 years he has explored the Desolation Wilderness, systematically fishing each of its 100 plus lakes.

Dedication

To my wife Danielle, who suffered all those dusty trails; to my uncle George, who taught me fly fishing at age 12; and to Mel Krieger, who finally got me to cast straight at age 44.

Introduction

Organization of the Guide

In addition to the Introduction, this guide is organized into seven chapters, each referring to a particular section of the Desolation Wilderness. In general the sections follow main stream drainages with specific information about each fishable lake in that drainage. Since most trails follow these streams there will be little information about hiking other than to mention the appropriate trails.

Several excellent topographic maps are available for the area. The map to have is the *Guide to the Desolation Wilderness* produced by the Forest Service. This recent (1990) creation is highly detailed with a two inch to the mile scale and 40 foot contours. It is hard to get lost using it. There are also excellent hiking guides available. The best is probably Robert Wood's *Desolation Wilderness,* but this book appears to be out of print. Its detailed treatment of cross-country routes is worth a library search. Less detailed but more up-to-date and currently available is Jeffrey Schaffer's *Desolation Wilderness and the South Lake Tahoe Basin.*

History

It is important to note at the start that the Desolation Wilderness represents a large and complex fishery with a long history. The geology of the area was ideal for producing small glacial lakes in granitic basins. There are over 100 such lakes and numerous streams. In the earliest days there were rainbow trout in Rockbound Valley descended from steelhead in the Rubicon River. There were also the Lahontan cutthroat trout of Lake Tahoe, which worked their way up tributaries into Fallen Leaf, Cascade and Floating Island Lakes. Man, of course, encouraged movement of fish into barren areas of the Wilderness even in the last century with the first recorded planting occurring in Gilmore Lake in 1887. A major effort was made by members of the Mount Ralston Fish Planting Club (MRFPC), formed in 1925, who over the following years planted over 100 locations in the Wilderness. This group also built modest stream flow dams on 23 lakes to stabilize water flow in creeks below lakes so that fish might survive dry summers and spawn when the lowest flows occur in the fall. Finally, modern management began in the 1950s when the California State Department of Fish and Game (DFG) began planting by aircraft.

In the last few years attention has focused on whether such planting has been a good idea in the overall management of Wilderness. Issues raised have included whether or not planting contributes to overuse and whether or not trout have had an adverse effect on certain native amphibian populations in the Sierra such as the Mountain Yellow-legged Frog. Despite such concerns there has been little hard data gathered about the biology of these fisheries and man's impact. The hope is that any proceeds from this guide will be used to foster the beginnings of studies which may shed some light upon these issues.

The Species

Until the stocking efforts of DFG the Desolation was basically an eastern brook trout fishery. Although today the most common species remains the brook trout, there are now a wide variety of fish, both wild and stocked, in the Wilderness. A useful reference for those interested in more information about species from a genetic and biological perspective is *Trout Biology* by Bill Willers.

Brook Trout

The most likely candidate for the species of fish you have just caught is a brook trout. This "trout" is not really a trout but a "char" and is native to the eastern United States and Canada. There are many different wildly-colored char found in Arctic waters. The fish is dark green or blue-black on the back, fading to white on the belly. Male bellies may turn a brilliant red in spawning season. The most distinguishing feature of this trout is its upper body markings, which are worm-like or mottled. Spots on the side may be yellow or pink with blue halos. These are light spots on a dark background. The lower fins, including the tail, have distinctive white leading edges. The tail is squared off—not forked.

The main feature of the brook trout which led to its wide introduction in the Desolation is its ability to spawn in lakes without tributaries, which all the rest of its relatives listed below require. The particular strain of brookie inhabiting the Sierra was developed by Seth Green in the 1800s and is noted for its early sexual maturity, which has led to an overpopulation of some lakes. Overpopulated lakes produced stunted fish with small bodies and oversized heads. One does not catch and release in such lakes. It is rather hard to overfish a brookie lake. Luckily, these are probably the best tasting of the Sierra trout.

Rainbows

The rainbow trout is native to some areas of Rockbound Valley. It can be identified most readily by the pink streak on its side; however, this characteristic is variable and may fade in lake bound fish which become more silvery such as those in Lake Tahoe. Steelhead are ocean-run rainbow trout. The back of the rainbow is usually olive to greenish blue, and the belly is white. Irregular spots are found on back, sides, head, dorsal fin and tail. These are dark spots on a light background. Some lakes in the Desolation have been consistently planted with rainbows, and they have done well.

Goldens

The golden is similar to the rainbow trout but has developed an incredible color scheme while living in isolation in some small streams in the southern Sierra. It readily interbreeds with the rainbow and rapidly loses its color. Apart from the striking colors, usually olive at the back fading to gold at the flanks and crimson on the belly, two identifying features are useful. First, it usually retains parr marks throughout life. Parr marks are large dark blotches, about a dozen or so, along the flanks covering about a quarter to a third of the width of the side. Goldens also have fewer spots on their sides than rainbows, usually not going more than halfway down the side, though the tail is usually full of spots. They can be mistaken for brookies if one looks only at the white edges on the lower fins.

Browns

The brown is not native to California, or North America for that matter, but is a European import. Its major characteristic is a brown to olive back with lighter brown on the sides. Its spots are usually larger than any other trout and are brown, black and red. Spots can be surrounded by halos of blue gray. The adipose fin, the one between the dorsal (top) fin and the tail, usually has an orange border. Lake dwelling browns develop a lighter coloring and may look similar to their relative, the Atlantic salmon.

Miscellaneous

At one point Stony Ridge and Gilmore Lakes were planted with lake trout or mackinaw. It is a large char, like the brookie, but with gray color. Its tail is forked, unlike the square-tailed brook trout. This is a very unlikely catch.

There have been some cutthroats planted into a few lakes, e.g., Dick's and Hidden. These basically look like rainbows but have a little red "slash" below the lower jaw.

Strategy

Whether one spin fishes or fly fishes, understanding which lakes to fish, when to fish the lake and where fish are most likely to be found in a lake are essential. Probably the most useful works on these topics are *Sierra Trout Guide* by Ralph Cutter and *Lake Fishing with A Fly* by Ron Cordes and Randall Kaufmann. They make several important points.

Which Lakes to Fish

Let's face it, some lakes clearly have better fisheries than others. One of the purposes of this guide is to help you find the better ones. The exact status of these lakes will change, and clever advice one month will be a big mistake the next. It is wise to have some idea of the factors which go into making an excellent fishery in the

Sierra and choose intelligently, regardless of the published wisdom.

Distance from civilization makes some difference, but in the Desolation, one is never really far from a trailhead. Nonetheless, it is a general rule that on most trails the first lake is hit the hardest. More important is getting off the trail a bit. Phipps Lake has excellent fishing only a couple hundred yards from the Tahoe-Yosemite Trail, but it is not *on* the trail. Altitude climbed works against you as the highest lakes often have the smallest food base upon which to build a trout population. Few of the higher more desolate lakes are worth fishing.

In general the lower the lake the better the feed and the bigger the fish. Clearly lakes with good weedbeds are an excellent potential source of insects. Trout will grow big in other lakes like Heather, which has a sparse weedless alpine character but has large numbers of redside shiners. Finally, the larger the lake, the larger the food base and the bigger fish can grow.

When to Fish the Lakes

The time of day generally has much less to do with fishing success than one might imagine. Clearly on most lakes there is a feeding period just after sunset and just before sunrise. One problem with these periods is that often every fish is feeding, including the runts. It is very difficult to cast to Moby Dick if he is surrounded by a dozen aggressive but small bodyguards. It is important to realize that if trout only ate at sunrise and sunset they would starve. They are in a sense always eating. They have to be opportunistic. So do not ignore high noon even for browns. Browns are notoriously nocturnal, but I have seen them tearing up the shiner population at high noon at Crag Lake. When hunger strikes, they raid the refrigerator.

More important than time of day is the time of year. One can be very successful if one is either the first or last angler to a lake during any season. The ideal time to get in is when there is a partial ice covering of the lake. The big problem is that in the spring ice on lakes may melt before snow on trails does, so you cannot get in at the right time. Furthermore, in spring more damage is created to trails and lakesides by trampling the wet ground. The fall may be a better choice as long as it does not snow before mid-November. It is very hard to get the timing correct. Chuck Yaeger solved this problem by overflying the Golden Trout Wilderness in an F-16 to check out the lakes before he hit the trails. Most of us do not have that option. A good thing to do is to keep some notes on your maps or guides about the exact days you went where. This is a general guide for next year. The other thing is to carefully consider the orientation of trails. Those with southern exposure clear first. Finding a good lake at the end of a trail with a southern exposure means early and late season access.

If one does have to fish for one week in mid-August, what's one to do? Probably the most important thing is to be prepared to fish deep. The fish are still there, down where the temperature is comfortable. This does not mean the deepest portion of a 100' deep lake. These areas are generally without oxygen and devoid of fish. The fish are 20 to 30' down in a comfortable stratum, and they are located where that stratum hits the submerged shore. They move in and out from there to forage. So in August, don't fish the shallows and don't fish the deeps, fish in between. Finally, in mid-summer you may be wise to go to a lake with rainbows as they still feed in the shallows in summer when the brookies and goldens are hiding.

Reading a Lake

The most important thing to do when one approaches a lake for the first time is to control the impulse to start fishing immediately. You probably do not have an unlimited amount of time available. Use it to your maximum advantage. Take a few seconds to figure out where to spend your efforts. When checking out the lake stay several feet from shore to prevent being spotted and use polarized sunglasses to help see the fish.

The inlet stream is usually my first choice for fishing a lake. This area is like an air-conditioned buffet line for the fish. The inlet brings in well-oxygenated water, perhaps cooler in the summer, and usually contains insects. Access may be a problem. This is a good reason to use float tubes. Outlets also may concentrate surface insects, but they are generally tougher to fish than inlets. The water may be shallow and lack cover for fish. Outlets usually lack a channel.

Channels may be either old flooded stream beds or areas that receive high flow during spring run-off. Fish are usually oriented in a channel as in a regular stream, i.e., facing upstream. In the channel one wants to work upstream from a position where it is harder for fish to spot you. If there is not much flow, fish still congregate in channels for cover and coolness in the summer.

Shallows will often hold much food, but there may be little cover to hide fish. These areas are often productive as sunset provides the cover of darkness. A big problem is approaching the fish without causing them to scatter. This may be impossible, and one may have to sit and wait until they return. One sure thing is that if there is food, they will come back. Remain stationary and become part of the

background decorations, as long as you do not dress like a rock star.
  Shoals are shallow areas surrounded by deeper water. If you can find them, they often have fish in the environs. Looking at a lake with polarized sunglasses in the morning before the wind comes up may allow you to see shoals not readily apparent later in the day.
  Springs are also wonderful if you can find them. Fish will congregate around them for "air conditioning" during the summer, bait fish also like them. At times they are very hard to find, but a few things help, such as a sandy bottom or bubbles. In the Sierra there is another type of spring, which is really an inlet stream that is flowing subsurface under conditions of reduced flow, i.e., the summer. If there is water flowing out of a lake and there is no obvious inlet, think springs.
  Shoreline weeds or sunken weedbeds usually offer a good chance to find feeding fish—the problem is the approach. Again, a float tube is helpful. Sometimes one can get into position on a point or log that overlooks a weedbed and cast around the edges of the weeds. Drop offs near weeds, shallows or other obvious feeding areas are worth attention. Clearly fish can stay on the deep side of the drop off and watch for food from a position of safety.

Float Tubes

  Now that you have heard a bit about all the places fish hide in a lake, it probably has become clear that you cannot get near most of them without a float tube. Unfortunately they cost a lot and they weigh a ton. I have tried thin walled tubes which allegedly you can inflate without a bicycle pump. I also watched one of these disintegrate underneath me in a chilly lake. You do not want to be in the middle of a lake when one of these falls apart. Also they will not last long.
  A standard tube weighs a considerable amount, but they can easily be placed on a frame pack for hiking in. It is useful to buy a frame extender, which adds an extra inverted U-shaped bar to the top of the frame. This allows much easier attachment with straps with real tethers (not the bungee cord type).
  You can save space by taking float tubes in deflated, but then one has to carry a bicycle pump. There is an important trick if one does this: carry a valve remover (they are built into the tops of many caps for covering inflation points). To inflate remove the valve, use lung power to get much of the initial air in, replace the valve, and do the last bit with the pump. Taking the valve out temporarily speeds deflation. *The Skillful Tuber* by Robert Alley has many useful hints.

Probably the most useful hint that I have learned from Alley is to carry two fly rods. Actually, you can easily identify people who have read the book by the two rods they have on their tubes. Ninety percent of the time one will be fishing from the tube with a sinking line, but the 10 percent of dry fly action will be missed unless one is prepared. Trying to change a spool in a float tube is a good 10-minute operation. By the time it is completed the rising fish are invariably gone. Carrying a dry fly set-up while fishing deep allows you to quickly change gears.

Finally, some of us are simply not going to be physically able to carry a float tube, camping equipment and fishing equipment into the Wilderness. One should not forget that there are packers available who can help. In most areas of the Desolation one can employ a packer to spot equipment at a certain site for a modest cost. The tremendous advantage of this is that one can take more equipment than one might otherwise. It opens the back country for those who for various reasons cannot carry a large load. My wife has a bad back and cannot carry any load. Having a packer help is better than my trying to carry two loads plus all of my fishing toys. Experienced packers who can help include those of the Camp Richardson Corral (916-541-3113) and Cascade Stables (916-541-2055). You may also get the latest fishing tips from these folks.

Tactics and Tackle

Spin Fishing

A basic issue is whether or not to use bait. On long trips it is virtually impossible to bring any live bait such as worms. Bringing any type of minnow into the back country is not only impractical but severely prohibited—putting such fish into new lakes may lead to competition for limited food supplies and ultimately hurt the trout. Newer cheese type baits tend to melt and make a mess in the heat of the outdoors. Finally, the major problem with bait is that it makes releasing the fish virtually impossible if it is swallowed. Though you may catch fish with bait, most will be small, and a fatally wounded four-inch trout is not worth much to anyone.

In general, lures are much more effective than bait. Not only will you catch more fish, you will catch bigger ones and you retain the option of releasing fish. More important than selection of the hot lure is bringing a selection of both types and sizes. The old standbys are the Mepps, Kastmaster, Rooster Tails, etc. If the lure is not working, vary the type, size and speed of retrieval. This is especially true if you see fish follow the lure but not take it.

The big limitation of lures is that they imitate only one type of food source, in general, bait fish. Reading below about fly fishing you will see there are many other types of food available for fish in lakes. Fly fishing is expensive and takes time to learn. A way to get in on the advantages of fly fishing with only spin tackle is to use clear plastic bubbles with flies. These types of floats provide enough weight to allow you to cast a weightless dry fly. Using models that can be filled with water allow you to present a wet fly. The water in the bubble provides weight to cast, but it sinks slowly, allowing you to retrieve the wet fly properly.

Finally, the lighter the tackle the better. First of all, you don't break your back hauling it in. Second, in terms of scaring fish, throwing a heavy spinner or weighted bait into a lake is similar to throwing a rock. Third, the heavier equipment requires stronger line which is easier for trout to see. Last of all, fish are more fun to play on the light tackle.

Fly Fishing

As with spin gear, the lighter the fly tackle the better. In general, 6 weight rods are getting into overkill and make a delicate presentation more difficult. A 5 weight rod is probably the standard. Lighter rods may be useful in situations where a delicate presentation is anticipated. Heavier rods, however, may be useful in situations where one expects to need to punch a fly into a gale or one needs to present heavier flies such as large streamers. For those who cannot make up their minds there is clearly one solution: bring two rods. A heavier rod is useful for underseas operations, i.e., flinging a sinking line, a heavy streamer and dealing with Moby Dick once he's on. The lighter rod is useful for delicate surface operations. Remember it's very nice to have two rods on a float tube.

Lines for fishing in mid-summer should include the fast sinking variety. You will need to get deep. The faster you do this, the more time in the target zone. If you plan to be working mostly in the shallows a sink tip is in order; otherwise you will be dredging the slimy bottom all day. It is wise to consider taking more than one type of sinking line. Using a terminal loop system will allow one to change sinking tips. Orvis markets a system to do this including loop attachments for the leader end of the fly line. This can also be accomplished with homemade arrangements which allow you to add sinking tippets to meet specific conditions. Remember, there are no fly shops in the middle of the Wilderness, so bring some alternative methods of changing sink rate of line.

What flies to take? It is very clear that for certain lakes cited, such as Heather, you will be completely naked without streamers, i.e., shiner imitations. The Black Nose Dace works quite well, though the shiners in the Desolation have a red streak. Sizes 8 or 10 are fine. Other streamers also work well and as in the case of the spin fisher, it is best to have a variety of types and sizes. Woolly Buggers are also a requirement for a venture into the Desolation. The color is not as important as the variety. Those tied with a small amount of tinsel seem to have added value. Woolly Buggers imitate a number of different food types besides shiners—leeches and worms. In addition a variety of small scud and damselfly imitations are of use in some lakes, for example, scuds for Cup and damselflies for Triangle.

Terrestrials are extremely important in the Desolation. Winds from the Central Valley bring in a wide variety of insects. The essentials are the ants, including carpenter ants. After Fourth of July grasshopper imitations are a must. These do not have to be the finely tied (expensive) sort. Reasonable approximations suffice.

It is well beyond the scope of this guide to go into the subtleties of insect hatches in the Desolation's lakes and streams. This topic has been covered in detail in a number of publications, the most relevant of which is Cutter's work which has a convenient chart of the basic hatches to be expected over the season. It is going to be a rare day, however, in the Desolation during which one will see cloud-like mayfly hatches and use many dries. We are primarily talking nymphs here. In terms of the basic nymphs to cover typical contingencies one would expect to have Zug Bugs, Bird's Nests and Pheasant Tails in sizes 12-18. You may also want to carry some small (size 20) Black Midge pupas. One does not see many stoneflies, but there are extensive damselfly hatches in some lakes, for example, Lake Of The Woods. The one dry fly that is absolutely essential is the Elk Hair Caddis in sizes 12-18. The second essential type of dry would be some small dark midges, sizes 18-24. Finally, an assortment of Parachute Adams would cover additional unpredictable situations.

Cordes and Kaufmann's work is exhaustive on the detail of the use of nymphs in a lake but to get started a good rule is that if you think you are doing a slow retrieve, cut your speed in half. In general you are trying to imitate an emerging larval form which starts at the bottom of the lake and rises to the top. Allow your offering to sink, then slowly draw it upward. There are untold hundreds of variations to this basic idea. One exception would be the midge pupa, which is fished in the film at the surface and allowed to drift. Expect takes to be soft. Leaders must be fine—6X. Setting the hook must be an exercise in delicacy, but you will be getting fish with nymphs. Getting the fish on the reel quickly, a light drag, and keeping your hands off the line, spool and handles will help in landing the fish. Remember, these are basically pretty small fish and one does not have to horse them around to land them.

Wilderness Permits and Ethics

Wilderness Regulations and Ethics

When I first started going into the back country in the 1960s, regulations were rare. They still are despite over 200,000 visitors to the Desolation each year. The permit system simply insures that you are less likely to see campers when you are overnighting. It also provides the Forest Service with data on use patterns. Day permits are available at most trailheads, but overnight permits must be obtained from a ranger station. The two most convenient are on Highway 50 near Placerville (916-644-6048) and in South Lake Tahoe (916-573-2600). If you are planning to stay overnight, call ahead of time and determine the best way to get a permit for your trip.

You must have one of these permits. Not having one virtually insures you will run into a back country ranger who at best will send you back to the trailhead and at worst will write you a ticket (yes, a ticket!) and then send you back to the trailhead. Another potential high point of your trip would be to have the same ranger check you for a fishing license which you "forgot." A final boost for your trip would be for that ranger to find you next to an illegal campfire. Gas stoves are permitted in the Wilderness (with a fire permit), but please familiarize yourself with the rules on fires before you leave. The reason fires are now outlawed was that the rangers were spending an incredible amount of time cleaning fire pits—campers pretended they were garbage disposals and foot-deep layers would accumulate in one season. All these regulations are described in detail on the back of the Forest Service map of the area, which is available at the ranger stations.

Now, there are some of us who react unfavorably to regulations, permits and the like. I have to admit there was a lot to be said for the good old days, but most can live with regulations when they understand their rationale. When entering the Desolation for the first time I am sure many are impressed by issues of how to preserve it. Learning how to preserve the wilderness requires knowledge of regulations. Even more important is making the ethical decision to follow the rules and to go beyond them. Just following the permit law may prevent a ticket, but in the long run the Wilderness will still suffer under the relentless pressure of visitors. There are many suggestions for good back country practice which require some effort, but if we follow these suggestions we take a step to preserve the area without ruining it. Below are listed a few such suggestions and their reasoning.

There are several suggestions for good back country practice upon which many of us agree—see the work by Cole for a solid review. First of all, prevent the proliferation of unsightly campsites. We should stick to the established campsites at most lakes. The lakes which get any use already have multiple campsites. These spots have clearly been used for decades and look it. There is little point in trying to establish a new campsite and destroy more of the environment. Usually the sites that have been established are the best ones anyhow. Paradoxically, it may be better to use a virgin campsite rather than one only slightly used. Your using that slightly used campsite will lead to its further downfall. If you are clever about using a virgin site, no one will ever see that it has been used before.

Second, regarding trails: like campsites, it's generally best to stick to established trails—the alternative is usually lost time. On established trails please stay in single file to prevent development of meandering systems of braided trails. If you have to go cross-country, do not travel in single file—spread out. This prevents the establishment of new trails and the destruction of untouched lands.

Third, we must carry out anything we bring in. One related sin anglers often commit is to throw fish viscera into lakes. These cold waters cause slow decay, and the unsightly leftovers may often be seen a month after the fact. You don't have to carry them out! Better to scatter the viscera on land where they quickly decay.

Fourth, choose clothing and equipment that blends into your surroundings so that you will be less obvious to others seeking solitude—both other campers and fish! Try to choose a campsite that is not obviously seen.

Fifth, for several easily imagined reasons, one should camp at least a hundred feet from the side of a lake or stream. Finally, there are a number of ethical issues related to fishing.

The stream between Upper and Lower Velma Lakes.

Cathedral Lake as the ice melts in early spring.

Granite Lake and Tahoe as seen from the Bayview Trail.

Float tubing for rainbows using damselfly imitations in Triangle Lake.

The stream between Upper and Lower Velma Lakes.

Float tubing among the rocks on the southeast shore of Middle Velma Lake.

The most common fish of the Desolation, the colorful brook trout.

A good brown surprised in the shallows of Crag Lake.

Streamside spawning soap opera; as the female waits in the background, two male brookies fight it out for her attention.

Shoreline of Granite Lake—home to brookie fry.

The cascading inlet stream to Desolation Lake.

Fishing Ethics

Catch and release fishing should be practiced where there are limited resources. About 60 percent of the lakes in the Desolation support brook trout which naturally reproduce. It is very hard to take too many of these from such lakes and in certain cases there is overpopulation, such as at Saucer Lake, which results in stunting. This is no reason for taking more than one can eat, particularly larger fish. Leaving a few will allow them to grow and get to the size many of us would really appreciate catching. This is particularly important for the 10 percent or so of lakes in which there are reproducing browns. These fish can grow to a large size if we let them.

Finally, some of the lakes of the Desolation cannot support a fish population without planting since they do not have trout which can reproduce in their waters. An example of this would be the rainbows of Middle Velma Lake. One can argue that you might as well take as many fish as you want from this lake since they are routinely replaced by DFG. I would still argue that fish should be returned to such lakes to allow them to get to a larger size. Why not share the trophy?

Releasing fish is next to impossible when using bait, especially when you catch small ones. Fly anglers have learned that barbless hooks or hooks on which the barb has been crimped down actually hold better than barbed hooks in most situations. The reason for this is that the smaller diameter of the hook point bites deeper and cleaner. Many fish caught with barbed hooks get off simply because the barb only allows the hook to get in to its barbed tip. As long as moderate tension is kept on the line, a fish will not get off a barbless hook unless he can swim backwards.

Releasing the fish itself should be accomplished with wet hands firmly gripping just above the tail and not crushing the fish's internal organs. Gently cradle the upper body while keeping your fingers out of the gills. Some fish may need to be helped in the water before they can swim off safely. Don't allow them to fall over upside down—they'll never right themselves. Hold them upright, moving them gently so that water moves through the gills. If you want to take a picture, keep the fish in the water until the photographer is ready and only raise the fish briefly.

Finally, we cannot take trout of any source in these lakes for granted. It is important to know that some would say that it is unethical to plant wilderness areas at all or even to foster wild trout propagation in any of these lakes or streams. Despite the long history of fishing by both settlers and native populations in the Tahoe

Basin, before 1900 most of the high country lakes in the Desolation were barren of fish. It has been argued that planting and fostering of wild trout where they did not live prior to the 1850s is "unnatural" and that furthermore trout may eat endogenous amphibians such as frogs.

You should know that planting has been stopped in the National Parks of California. Will this happen in the official wilderness areas? I hope not. Having essentially grown up in back country areas I have always felt that at least during my lifetime fishing has always been an integral part of that back country experience. I would hope that the National Parks of California can be left to those who would preserve the original state of the Sierra, but, I hope that we can learn enough to allow fishing to continue in other wilderness areas with minimal impact on the environment. These issues are currently under serious debate by various State and Federal agencies. That we will always be able to fish in the California Sierra should not be taken for granted. It may turn out to be a privilege we have to fight to preserve.

Main Lakes of Each Section of the Desolation Wilderness

Section 1: Echo Lakes

The Echo Lakes are outside the Wilderness proper, but the entrance road to the lakes from Highway 50 provides easy access to the back country. The real claim to fame for this access is that it starts at over 7,400' so that there is little need to gain more altitude. This entrance is made even more attractive by the Pacific Crest Trail along the north shore of the Echo Lakes. Due to its overconstruction the Trail has been described as the Santa Monica Freeway of the High Sierra. There is also a pleasant lodge at the start of the trail (Echo Chalet). Finally, to attract even more visitors there is a water taxi running from the end of the road two or three miles to the end of the upper lake. Using this entrance, one gets a running start at getting into the Sierra. This fact has not been missed by the hiker and angler and the area is heavily infested with both. Nonetheless, there are interesting lakes in this area which escape the masses.

Cup Lake

This lonely lake probably offers the best chance for the novice to catch a moderate sized golden trout in the Wilderness. One look at a topo map will show why: it is virtually unvisited. Although it is located only 1.5 miles or so from either Upper Echo Lake or Highway 50 below Phillips (Pow Wow), it is at the 8,600' level of a very steep mountain. Access can be attempted from Highway 50 up 1,700' of scree (rock) slopes. One stays to the east of a small spur. This route is only for those familiar with navigating loose rock.

The approach from Echo Lakes is more civilized if one can get the water taxi to drop you at Dartmouth Cove. From here a trail leads to Saucer Lake. One starts this climb at 7,400' which is 600' higher than the Route 50 approach. One climbs from Saucer Lake to a ridge to its south then west to overlook and descend to Cup. The problem with this approach is the descent, which again is over scree, and the depressing fact that one has to go back up to regain the ridge when leaving Cup. A final issue is that unless you make careful arrangements you will find no water taxi waiting for you when you return to Dartmouth Cove. This leads to a long walk around Echo to return to your car. In either case, getting to Cup is an adventure but one that can be accomplished in a single day.

Cup Lake has been air stocked with goldens since the 1960s. There were earlier plants of brookies, but they do not seem to have been successful. I have taken fish up to 14" here. They seem to have the unusual food source of some freshwater shrimp. The flesh of these fish is bright red, quite different from that of other lakes. The taste is exotic.

The most important point of strategy for this lake is to arrive at the right season, either early spring or late fall. The fish are clearly feeding at these times and are near the surface and in the shallows. In the summer the fish scatter and are found in deeper water, virtually inaccessible.

The big problem with selecting the spring and fall seasons to visit is the unpredictability of the weather. I have found the lake starts to freeze over about November 10th. This, however, will vary by season. A wild card in visiting the lake is snow. Any appreciable snowfall makes the trip impossible since one cannot move safely over boulder fields half covered with snow. Light snow burns off on the south facing slope above Highway 50 so this really is the most likely approach. My experience with spring is that by the time the snow melts, so has the ice on the lake, and it is not worth the trip.

Saucer Lake

The access to this lake has already been described in reference to a trip to Cup. This lake in and of itself is not worth the effort of the climb. It almost led to a divorce in my family. However, if you poop out on the way to Cup, at least there are some fish to be had at Saucer.

Goldens have been stocked in this lake since the 60s but do not seem to have done well. There is a surviving population of brookies. The brookies are perhaps the best (worst) example of stunted trout I have seen in Desolation. Apparently the meals are few and far between here, and anglers do not cull the population. The air drops of golden fingerlings once a year must seem like CARE packages. If you do fish this lake, please keep a few fish.

There is nothing unusual about Saucer in fishing strategies other than I would not like to make the approach early in the season when the north facing trail is likely to be very wet, if passable at all.

Triangle Lake

The easy way to get to Triangle Lake is clearly the Pacific Coast Trail from Echo Lakes, which makes for a very pleasant day hike with little altitude gain. There is also access from the Fallen Leaf Lake area via a trail which departs the road just before Lily Lake. This hike is a death march and not to be recommended unless one is marooned at Fallen Leaf Lake for longer than a week and is desperately seeking some fishing. This lake has been stocked with both rainbows and brookies, though it has only received rainbows since 1970. They grow rapidly, maximum size is about 12-14 inches.

Unfortunately for spin anglers, Triangle Lake is weedy. One could probably stock a sporting goods store with the snagged lures on the bottom. There is also a large log right in the middle—seen from the hills on a calm day. Fly fishers should strongly consider a float tube as there is very little backcasting room. The lake is small enough that roll casts can get a long way proportionately into the lake, but a tube is still best. There is one area which supports full fly casts near the point where the trail meets the lake. Do not visit here without damselfly nymphs and adults.

Lost Lake

This lake can be part of a trip to Triangle. A topo is necessary to find it, though it is close by. The easiest way to find it is suggested by Wood: from the point on the Triangle Lake Trail that you first see Triangle Lake turn left and contour over (move left and do not change altitude), and the lake is within a quarter mile. Alternatively one can see the course of the Lost Lake outlet stream from Triangle Lake (a line of trees) and work your way over. Both these routes are off-trail and can easily lead to a broken ankle for the unfamiliar.

This is another brook trout stronghold which receives regular feedings of golden fingerlings, care of DFG. The lake has a good food supply of brookies and the fish are nicely developed. I have yet to catch a golden here. One might find out if they exist in the spring if they go through the motions of spawning in the small inlet stream.

This lake is small and shallow in most parts except very conveniently right in front of a large boulder at the nearest point to the Triangle Lake Trail. Casting from this area with fly or spin gear is feasible and it provides an excellent picnic spot.

Tamarack Lake

This name is really a misnomer as the true tamarack pine (Larix or Eastern Larch) does not live in California. Often the lodgepole *(pinus murrayana)* is referred to as a tamarack pine and this is probably the source of the name.

The lake is easy to reach from the Pacific Crest Trail. Unfortunately, since it is so easy to reach the shore line has been heavily overused at the point where the trail meets the lake. For that reason alone I put this lake low on my list of attractions. There are, however, other good campsites around the lake. This is a brook trout fishery. The best hope in this lake is inlet area strategy, though access is easy along most of the shoreline and there is room for fly fishing along the southwest shore.

Ralston Lake

Ralston Lake is named after William Chapman Ralston, a prominent financier of gold-rush days. It is right next to Tamarack Lake and is a pleasant visual alternative, especially given its striking alpine setting. This lake has received both brookies and rainbows and they attain moderate size. This is a large lake with deep cuts near shore. A float tube would be extremely useful for cruising the edge. A particularly interesting spot is just across the stream outlet dam where a bluff enters the water.

Through a set of lucky circumstances I met the person who constructed this dam, Haven Jorgensen, who now in his 80s is one of the few surviving members of the Mount Ralston Fish Planting Club (MRFPC). Jorgy was once the owner of Echo Chalet and in his retirement still climbs up to Saucer Lake to check on the status of the golden plants. This dam was the last constructed in the area and is in some disrepair due to Jorgy's attempt to use less mortar between the stones to give the dam a more natural appearance. This dam provides enough consistent flow into Echo Lakes to provide spawning for its residents. Jorgy notes that the clever angler can find trout all along this stream and in particular along the small stretch of stream down to Cagwin Lake.

Cagwin Lake

Cagwin is just downstream from Ralston and is named after the Hermit of the lake, Hamden "El Dorado" Cagwin, a hunter and fisherman who settled on Lower Echo Lake in 1896. The Hermit was an accomplished snowshoer and carried the mail from Strawberry to Carson City. This smallish lake has received primarily rainbows, but you can bet there are also brookies from upstream. Much of Cagwin is shallow and not prime territory except for the southwest rocky shore, where there are deeper areas near drop-offs.

Section 2: Desolation Valley

The Desolation Wilderness, created in 1966, takes its name from this valley. Originally it was called the "Devil's Valley" in the 1880s. Conservation of the area began in 1910 with the creation of the El Dorado National Forest, followed by designation of the Desolation Valley Wild Area in 1931. Access to this area is either up the Horsetail Falls Trail from Twin Bridges on Highway 50 or across from Lake Of The Woods and the Echo Lake area. Going up the Horsetail Falls Trail with a full pack is an experience not likely to be repeated. In crucial areas it is no more than a rocky slope with cairns (stone piles which serve as trail markers—sometimes called ducks). If you really want to visit this area, the side route from Echo Lakes, though less direct, is much easier hiking with a full pack.

Although there are a number of unique lakes in this area, one really finds oneself wandering from tarn to tarn without caring much due to the spectacular scenery. The area is really the heart and soul of the Desolation. It is wide-open, full of small lakes, glacier-polished granite and peaks. It is an area to explore without a pre-planned itinerary.

Avalanche Lake

Really a wide spot in Pyramid Creek just above the falls, it serves as a rest stop for those who have survived the climb up the trail or as pause for reflection for those concerned about breaking a leg on the way down. This lake has received mostly rainbows, but the area above is teeming with brookies. Rainbows love fast water, and there is fast water here. In fact, fish that like such water just have to head downstream for the fast water ride of their lives. I would not go wading anywhere near the falls. One can sometimes see fish in the current within casting distance of the shore.

In this lake one fishes where there is the most current. Fly fishing is possible both with dries into the current or nymphs on a strike indicator or a dropper. The dropper technique allows one to fish a dry on top and a nymph below. There are several ways to attach the nymph. I prefer to tie an additional blood knot near the end of my tippet, leaving extra line on the tags. This allows you to attach two flies: you can either attach the dry on top, which allows the wet to drop to the same depth as the tag you have left, or you can attach the wet on top which allows the wet fly to remain near the surface in the film.

Pitt Lake

This is the next stop up the trail from Avalanche Lake. There are a number of little lakelets in this area, and the geography is confusing. Suffice it to say all the lakelets are part of the same complex and most have fish visible to the casual observer. Here stealth is important. You will usually see the fish before you cast. Light equipment and a delicate presentation are essential for both fly and spin fishing alike. Pitt, like Avalanche, has a current. A good place to find brookies is where the lake narrows. Fish congregate here as in a feeding lane in a stream. Fish may also be found next to the extensive weedbeds and in Pyramid Creek above the lake.

Ropi, Toem, Osma and Gefo Lakes

Many of the lakes of this area were unnamed when the Mount Ralston Fish Planting Club (MRFPC) began its work in the 1920s. The members gave the lake names an Indian flavor by using the first two or three letters of their first and last names, thus Ropi is from ROss PIerce. This operation worked better with some names than others. Toem Lake was named after Tom Emery of the MRFPC; Gefo after George Foss.

These lakes form a chain to the west above Ropi and provide pleasant brook trout fisheries. The highest of the chain, Gefo, though very attractive, is shallow and subject to winter kill. This is the death of fish during the winter, not due to freezing, but deoxygenation of the water. Toem usually has an excellent population regardless of the winter. It is only a few feet higher than Ropi and offers some good spots for fly casting. In Ropi, one should particularly check the well-oxygenated inlet area.

Pyramid and Waca Lakes

These lakes also drain into Ropi, but from the northwest. Access is via the Ropi-Toem-Gefo chain or from Lake Aloha. Named after Walter Campbell of the MRFPC, Waca Lake and Pyramid Lake are brookie lakes. Pyramid Lake should not be confused with the Pyramid Peak Lakes, which are on the other side of Pyramid Peak and are barren. Many of the tarns in the area are full of frogs and tadpoles. Green Woolly Buggers are effective in the two main lakes.

Desolation, Chain, Channel and American Lakes

This officially named chain of lakes are northeast of Ropi and are, as with the other chains of lakes, brookie fisheries. There have been plantings of rainbows sporadically in these areas, so one may be surprised. This particular area is one of the most pleasant places in the Wilderness to wander about fishing. There are many idyllic pools and channels, all with a certain number of fish. The biggest problem is getting lost or finding yourself on the wrong side of a channel from where you would like to be. One should not be in a rush to pass through.

The stream into American Lake deserves particular attention, not right where it enters the lake, but a bit further into the lake where it broadens and deepens. This is a feeding line with good shelter—a prime lie. Part of this area, between Chain (unnamed on the map) and Channel, resembles a formal Japanese garden and was so named by the Echo Lake cabin owners. Fish may be found throughout the area both in streams and lakes. The bottom lake, Desolation is easily linked to Lake Of The Woods cross-country or to Ropi down Pyramid Creek.

Lake Of The Woods

This is an extremely productive lake which would assure great fishing if it were not so close to civilization. Its shores are highly eroded from years of use by travelers, primarily from the Echo Lakes basin, which is the main access point to the rest of the lakes described in this section. Brookies have done better here than rainbows as plants, but both develop to good size due to the extensive feed available. There are wide weedbeds along the shores which provide both food and cover for the fish. Even in the middle of summer rainbows venture close to shore to feed, and they can be large. A float tube is very helpful to reach deeper water and to fish back towards the weedbeds.

Frata Lake

Named after Frank Talbot of the MRFPC, this lake provides a marginal brookie fishery and is shallow and subject to winter kill. It is overshadowed by its big neighbor described above. This lake is better for swimming than fishing.

Lake Aloha

The origin of this lake's name is unclear, since it is anything but a tropical setting. On a map this is the largest appearing lake in the Desolation, but it does not hold a huge amount of water. It was enlarged by a PG&E dam which allows the water to run out during the summer for the power company's purposes. Thus what may be an alpine landscape in spring turns to a lunar landscape by fall.

These shifts in depth are not good for fishing. It received extensive plants of both brookies and rainbows in the past. One trick to the lake is to wait to fish it until fall when the water level drops and the fish are more concentrated. Furthermore, one should examine the seldom visited rocky shoreline past the trail to Mosquito Pass.

Lake Lucille and Lake Margery

Lake Lucille is named after Lucille Meredith, a banker's wife of the early 1900s. These two shallow lakes are brookie fisheries. They are hard hit due to their proximity to the Pacific Crest Trail and the small trail that leads down to Grass Lake and Fallen Leaf Lake. They are not worth the hike from Fallen Leaf. If you really needs to fish one or the other, Lucille is better.

Lake Le Conte

This granite-bound lake is named after Professor Joseph Le Conte (1823-1901), a geologist who wrote extensively about glaciation in the High Sierra. The shore and setting demonstrate this glaciation and provide a scenic camping site. This lake has received both rainbows and brookies. These fish have not grown to any size, but they are readily available.

Jabu Lake

Named after Jack Butler of the MRFPC, this lake provides an incredible view of the Fallen Leaf area from its outlet stream. It has only been stocked with goldens. I have not been able to catch a fish here, but reports indicate that they exist but do not grow large. I suspect that I have been there at the wrong season. This lake provides a campsite slightly off the beaten path.

Section 3: Wright's Lake

The area around Wright's Lake receives much use. The blacktop road from Highway 50 brings many vacationers each year, yet there are a few places rarely visited in this area which afford some fine fishing. The road to Wright's Lake also affords access to the Barrett Lake jeep trail and more fishing in a different drainage.

Lyon's Lake

The Lyon's Lake trail is not heavily used but traverses some very pleasant forest. The stream which parallels the trail occasionally has a fish. Lyon's Lake is itself the largest lake on the trail and a fine goal for this five-mile walk. The lake is in a granitic valley and has a good population of resident brookies. The fish get large here but are not as easily caught as in Lake Sylvia. A prime spot for fishing is around the inlet stream, but this is best reached by float tube due to bushes. Other good areas include the boulder fields which enter the water next to the inlet stream. One can cast to the inlet area from rocks to either side, but the casts are long. There are also small fish that respond to a fly in the outlet stream and its lakelet.

Lake Sylvia

This lake is less used than Lyon's Lake but provides an extensive brookie fishery. The fish are on the verge of overpopulation but are not yet stunted. One can easily camp at either lake and fish both. Getting to this lake requires less altitude gain than getting to Lyon's Lake, but the setting, though quite nice, is not as spectacular. The inlet stream is a good spot, but there are fish throughout the lake.

This lake provides probably the shortest access point for those who want to try to climb Pyramid Peak. It is an excellent spot for parties including alpinists who don't fish. The view from the top of the Peak is unbelievable with the whole Wilderness spread out below.

Grouse Lake

The next trail in the Wright's Lake area leads from Wright's Lake to the east. It is heavily used, but there are fish, brookies especially, near the inlet stream. One alternative to the heavily used area of Grouse Lake is Secret Lake, which is directly south and also has brookies. This requires a cross-country jaunt.

Hemlock Lake

This small lake is named after the stand of mountain hemlock on the south shore. This is a pleasant, small lake with a good resident population of small brookies. Casting is a problem at times due to the brushy shore.

Smith Lake

The final destination of this trail, at 8,700', is alpine Smith Lake. This lake is larger than the two one passes on the way up and offers the most attractive campsites. It is heavily populated with brookies. According to Wood, alpinists may also be able to find a way to Lyon's Lake from here.

Twin Lake

The trail to Twin and Island Lakes branches off at a lower altitude from the Smith Lake trail and appears to get more use. I once saw a grandfather taking his grandchildren up here on the backs of some llamas. There are, however, some spots near here that may be a bit underused, such as the outlet steam from Island Lake. This goes into a little lakelet via some falls. Fish love this oxygenated water, especially in high summer. Boomerang Lake on the way to Island Lake also allegedly contains brookies, as may Umpa Lake to the northwest. There are possibilities for expeditions to hidden places even in this overused basin.

Island Lakes

These lakes were once stocked with goldens, but the resident brookies made short work of them and the planting was eventually stopped. This is a barren but striking alpine basin with a reasonable fishery. In his guide Robert Wood describes a cross-country route to Clyde Lake starting in this cirque. Looking at the headwall above the lake this adventure does not appeal to me.

Tyler Lake

The Rockbound Pass trail linking Wright's Lake and Rockbound Valley receives heavy use. The Tyler Lake offshoot is relatively less used and provides some interesting opportunities. On the way up watch at about the 7,860' level for the Tyler's grave lateral trail. This short trail is marked with an enameled sign which is easy to miss on the way up the trail but easier to see while descending. Tyler was a ranch hand who froze to death in an early season storm near the lake that bears his name. His grave is in a quiet dell about 100 yards off the main trail with a white marble military headstone. It is one of those places that gives the Wilderness some of its character. In any case, the lake is well supplied with brookies.

Gertrude Lake

This pleasant small lake slightly below Tyler is stocked with goldens. This provides a pleasant challenge for earlier and later in the season. One may also want to walk down the outlet stream to fish.

Maud Lake

It is hard to believe that one might find good fishing at this lake right on the autobahn between Wright's Lake and Rockbound Valley. Nonetheless, there are fish in the lake and, for fly fishers, also in the outlet and inlet streams. Using a stealthy approach one will find large fish, mostly brookies, hidden in undercuts of the inlet stream. These fish are not easy to approach but provide an insight to the size of fish that can live even in an overused lake like Maud. There are also fish in the outlet stream and in its lower reaches (the Jones Fork of Silver Creek reached from the Barrett Lake jeep trail) which appear to be mostly wild rainbows.

Barrett Lake

The hiker (or jeeper) can reach Barrett Lake via the Barrett Lake jeep trail from Dark Lake in the Wright's Lake area. This trail is virtually unused in early season before it is open to jeeps. Barrett Lake is outside the Wilderness, but this lake and its outlet stream provide good brook trout fishing.

Lawrence Lake

The first stop out of Barrett Lake is Lawrence Lake. This is a fine brookie fishery with fish of all sizes in quantity. They will congregate at the inlet stream from Top Lake. Lost (or Gem) Lake directly west of Lawrence Lake just inside the Wilderness, also provides brookie fishing off the beaten path. Lake Number 9, due east, is barren.

Top Lake

A fairly obvious trail leads from Lawrence up to Top Lake. This lake still receives golden plants but has a number of large brookies which appear to have been using the goldens as a vitamin supplement. There are fewer fish here than at Lawrence, but there are some large (read smart) ones. This lake provides some spectacular camp sites with views overlooking the Sacramento area. There is plenty of casting room for fly fishers, and nymphs work well.

Lake Number 5

The Red Peak Trail out of Barrett Lake leads to this swampy lake. It has a marginal brookie population and a massive mosquito population.

Section 4: Rockbound Valley

There are several obvious access routes into this area. Luckily for camping solitude, most of the routes involve enough distance to make day trips impossible.

Rockbound Lake

This lake's name dates to the last century, with Rockbound Pass dating to 1915. The Pass was designed as an emergency escape route for cattle in the event of an early snow. Access to this area is usually achieved via the jeep trail to Buck Island Lake, which is out of the Wilderness. The Rubicon Springs area on this jeep trail receives heavy use, but the old foot trail around the north side of Rockbound Lake and on to Fox Lake is quite unused. Hikers often enter via Loon Lake and the major trail beginning there. This trail is the old construction road for Rubicon Reservoir. There are still fish in the old outlet course to the Rubicon River from Rubicon Reservoir, but this area is a shadow of what it once was before the construction of the reservoir. There are browns, brookies and planted rainbows in this lake as well as some brookies in small, seldom-visited Fox Lake.

Rubicon Reservoir

This is a totally artificial addition to the Wilderness which flooded the old Onion Flat area (see old topos). There is no point in recounting the destruction of the Rubicon River as a wild trout stream by this construction in the late 1950s and early 1960s, but suffice it to say that the Rubicon used to have steelhead and was a world famous trout stream. It now runs wild (when there is water) for less than 10 miles into this reservoir. There are browns, brookies and rainbows. The proof that the Rubicon River is still wild is that one will catch rainbow-golden hybrids in it. Even in a dry year they may be found in pools. The fish share characteristics of both rainbow and golden trout.

Clyde Lake

The headwaters of the Rubicon start at Clyde Lake. This lake has plenty of goldens, and they stretch their way down the canyon where eventually they intermix with the rainbows moving up from Rubicon Reservoir. This is not to say that they are easy to catch. The lake is large, and the fish spread out during the summer when it is feasible to get there. Clyde Lake itself has an Arctic feel to it, especially in the spring and fall. It is surrounded by a huge cirque with many interesting cross-country routes on the rim well described in Wood's guide. This lake is most easily accessed from Lake Aloha and Mosquito Pass.

Lake Doris

This lake is actually two closely attached lakes which are in the high alpine valley on the northeastern side of Rockbound Pass. They are currently stocked with goldens but have held brookies in the past, and there are probably still some there. Fishing has never been good in this lake, possibly due to the altitude (8,400') and the likelihood that snow may fall heavily on this side of the Pass and lead to winter kill. Anglers should probably keep on walking past these lakes.

Lake Lois

Moving down from Rockbound Pass, one sees Lake Lois. This lake is much larger than its sister, Doris, and is a brook trout fishery. Camping sites are poor around the lake. It tends to be windswept, reducing its popularity with overnighters (who drop down into sheltered Lake Schmidell), but this lack of camping attention may be an advantage to the angler. There are many rocky points off which fish gather.

Lake Schmidell

This is a large, deep lake with an extensive brookie fishery. Fish come in all sizes and are plentiful. Particularly good areas to fish are the hard to reach inlet streams on the southwest corner of the lake. Of high interest to the catch and release fly fisher is the small lakelet just below the outlet dam. This lake is teeming with small (to six-inch) trout which take readily to the fly. There are plenty of good casting room and an attractive inlet stream which provides continuous action. In early morning and evening there are rises covering this lake.

Leland Lakes

These lakes are stocked with goldens, but the fish do not seem to do well. There are few fish in the upper lake. The edges of the lakes are shallow in most spots, and it is difficult to find fish in mid-season. Access to this area is difficult in the spring and fall. The shortcut that connects these lakes with Lake Schmidell mentioned by Wood in his guide is not worth the effort considering the good trail between the two areas. A general rule is three miles on a trail moves as quickly as one mile cross country—and without twisted ankles.

Zitella, Horseshoe and the 4-Q's Lakes

All of these lakes are shallow brook trout fisheries. I believe Zitella is subject to winter kill. These swampy areas are not particularly inviting, especially in early season with high water, wet ground and mosquitoes. Nonetheless, there is food for trout in some of these lakes, and you may be surprised by the size of some of the larger residents.

Highland Lake

This lake gets more use than one might imagine from its location on the trails. The secret is that many campers and packers go cross-country from a number of starting points, including the Tell's Peak Trail and Rubicon Reservoir. The lake does provide one of the better pure rainbow fisheries in the Wilderness. Fly fishers will be attracted to the outlet stream, which has a number of wild fish in its streambed and lakelets. Many of the lakelets in this wild area appear to have fish in them, possibly due to errant air plantings from DFG.

Section 5: Meeks Creek

This popular area receives heavy use. The Tahoe-Yosemite Trail is its thoroughfare, and it is built to high standards. This is generally an overnight use area since the first lake is 4.6 miles in with a 1,200' elevation gain. Some, however, do hike in for the day to the closest lakes. There are fish in Meeks Creek all along this trail, but, fishing is difficult due to heavy undergrowth. Where access is easy, habitat degradation has occurred through heavy human use (waders and swimmers). In many places getting to the stream requires a tank.

Lake Genevieve

This lake is the first stop, about 4.6 miles, up the Tahoe-Yosemite trail from Meeks Bay. Because it is the closest of the Tallent Lakes, it receives considerable attention from day hikers. It is primarily a brook trout fishery with some browns. It has received rainbows in recent years. One really needs a float tube to do this lake justice. The shorelines are shallow and extensive, making access to deeper waters where fish summer difficult.

Crag Lake

This the next lake up the trail from Genevieve. It is a total distance of slightly less than five miles from Meeks Bay. This lake sees few day hikers as they all seem to poop out at Genevieve 0.4 miles closer to the trailhead. There is a circuitous inlet stream channel from Hidden Lake which is substantially deeper than its surroundings. This channel goes along for a good 200 yards and is certainly worth careful examination. The outlet end of the lake is rather shallow and not a good bet. One will see browns cruising on the side of the lake opposite the main trail. These fish are looking for their primary food source, the red-sided shiners that abound in the lake.

This is not an easy lake to fish and is a good lake for novices to avoid. The browns have an unending food source and are suspicious of imitations. On the other hand, they are large fish.

Hidden Lake

This is the next lake up the trail from Crag, a total of about 5.4 miles from Meeks Bay. There is a spur trail from the main trail which leads down to it. One barely catches a glimpse of the lake from the main trail. This appears to be a pure brookie fishery. The outlet area is rather shallow and unappetizing. There are, however, several rocky points and ledges in the lake which attract its residents.

Shadow Lake

Just beyond the turn off to Hidden Lake is Shadow Lake. In early morning this lake is in the shadow of Rubicon Peak, hence the name. At this point one is about six miles in from the trailhead and really at the limit of feasible (gung-ho) day hiking. Those addicted to reading topo maps will notice that it is only about two miles in a straight line to this point from the end of the highest road at the development on Rubicon Bay just south of Lonely Gulch. This area, however, does not afford access to Shadow Lake as one cannot reach Forest Service land without trespassing on private property. In any case, this approach would be very difficult.

Shadow Lake itself is a reasonable brookie fishery with a few browns thrown in. It is shallow but has good sized fish. There is a convenient sand spit next to the inlet stream (in low water) which affords foot access to casting to the inlet stream as well as the lily pads at the entrance side of the lake.

Stony Ridge Lake

This large lake is sometimes called Upper Tallent Lake, but its current name is clearly derived from the 9,000' ridge, which includes Rubicon Peak and separates it from the Tahoe basin. Stony Ridge Lake has received all types of fish, including the first fish plant in the Desolation—mackinaws—in the late 19th century. The largest recorded here weighed 28 pounds, but there is little news of any recent catches of this species. The current species likely to be found are rainbows, brookies and browns. There is natural reproduction in the inlet stream.

The center of this lake is over 120' deep, beyond the range of my fish finder. In these deep areas there are few fish to be seen. For those who would like to try to get mackinaw, probably the best advice is to go out with a charter on Lake Tahoe. The definitive reference on mackinaw strategy is by Roush. He has never fished this lake but feels it still contains fish and states he would like to try jigging for them. I have seen large quantities of fish on my fish finder at depths consistent with mackinaw (50-60 feet) but had no success jigging.

The more likely successes in this lake are along the shore at the drop-offs. There are large numbers of fish in this lake, but they are difficult to reach without a float tube. A reasonable strategy from the western shore is to try to fish the drop-offs easily visible where the sandy beaches suddenly fall off to the depths. More rocky drop-offs are found on the eastern shore, and these can be reached with relatively short casts from that shore. There are redsided shiners in the lake, and fish move into the shallows for the shiners from the security of these drop-offs. One should also note that even when the inlet stream is dry there are springs in the inlet area which attract fish. Fish can also be found up this stream in early summer while there is still flow.

The tactics for fishing this lake are the usual except for those involving mackinaw. The necessities for the macs are: an inflatable boat or float tube, an early start since they appear to like to feed at daybreak, a fish finder to identify their depth and large flashy lures, flies or jigs.

Cliff Lake

This small lake is reached from Stony Ridge Lake by a moderate death march up the cross-country track that follows its brushy outlet stream. The lake has extensive cliffs to the southwest. Cliff Lake has innumerable small brookies. Prior attempts to plant goldens failed due to this population of cannibals. Access points are limited due to the terrain, but this does not matter as there are many (too many) small fish. At least all the rises in the evening are indeed trout and not shiners, as is the case on many other lakes. This is a pleasant camping area off the beaten track. Fish here do not get as large as those of Phipps Lake.

Rubicon Lake

This is a modest brookie fishery on the trail to Phipps Pass. It is hit rather hard by the passing masses and is a less sure bet than Grouse or Phipps Lakes.

Grouse Lakes

These two small lakes are a short distance from Rubicon Lake, but this is a long distance from the Meeks Bay trailhead (more than eight miles). Those who spend their winter hours looking at topos will probably have noticed that a gully leads directly up 1.5 miles from Eagle Lake (one mile from the Eagle Lakes trailhead). This distance is extremely deceptive as the gully is full of large boulders which require climbing skills and alternatives outside the gully require mazanita mountaineering skills of the highest degree. This gully is particularly dangerous to descend (a general rule in technical climbing is that it is easier to go up rocks than down), and one may be forced into some very unpleasant bushes. All in all this short approach is a route to avoid.

The Grouse Lakes are brookie lakes. The upper lake was full of up to 12-inch fish the last time I was there, but fish appeared on the verge of stunting and a bit eel-like. The small lower lake had fewer fish, but the ones I could catch were well-fed and larger than those of the bigger upper lake.

The upper lake has seen beaver activity, and their home provides a tenuous casting point for fly and spin anglers. If the lodge disappears some large boulders behind it allow casting access to a deeper area of the pond which appears to be the lair of its larger residents. The lower lake has some granitic shelves perfect for fly fishing back casts. The lower lake fish appear to be eating a variety of nymphs in some weedbeds, but on my last trip they seemed to want to fight over a streamer.

Phipps Lakes

General Phipps, a veteran of the Indian wars, settled at the mouth of General Creek near Sugar Pine Campground in Tahoma. His lakes with the peak above are well worth a visit. The upper lake is about nine miles from either the Eagle Lakes or Meeks Bay entrance. Do not be fooled by the short map distance up the gully from Eagle Lake (see notes on Grouse Lakes).

With two cars, one may make a pleasant loop hike up the Eagle Falls Trail past the Velmas and then down the Meeks Bay trail. On such a trip one will can see some of the most varied fishing in the Wilderness: rainbows in Middle Velma, brookies in Phipps and Grouse Lakes and browns in the Crag Lake area. Because this lake is off the trail—even though only a few hundred yards—it gets less use. Lower Phipps Lake may possibly be reached by a major bushwhacking adventure and has little to offer over the main lake.

This is an excellent brookie fishery. If one cannot catch them here, it is hopeless. The lake has also received stockings of goldens. In all the years I have been up here I have only gotten one of these. Again, I think the brookies eat the golden fingerlings. Fishing is quite the same all around the lake, although there is one excellent granitic shelf that affords casting room for fly fishing.

Section 6: Eagle Creek

The prime access to this area is via the Eagle Lakes Trail. With good reason few will use the Bayview Trail—dusty, steep, horse manure decorations. Access to the Snow Lake area on Cascade Creek is via Bayview Campground and the trail leading south from the parking lot. This trail becomes very much cross-country at times and probably receives five percent of the use of the Eagle Lakes Trail.

Eagle Lake

It may be hard to believe that the most heavily used trail and lake in the Wilderness was indeed once surrounded by wild eagle nests. In the distant past both golden and bald eagles nested in the high peaks surrounding this picturesque lake. There has been an attempt to reintroduce falcons along the north canyon wall. The lake itself receives rainbows but also has browns and brookies descended via the inlet stream.

The inlet stream area is the place to fish along with the area just to the north of the inlet. This can only be done well with a float tube. Surprisingly, there are many fish in these areas directly across from where the hordes visit the lake at the point where the trail arrives. One can fish with grasshopper imitations along the bush line and drop-off north of the inlet stream. Nymphs are also effective in the weedy areas bordering the inlet stream. Another interesting place is where the scree slope enters the lake on the north side. The center of the lake is over 80 feet deep and fishless. There is a little island which is a great place for a float tube picnic.

Lower Velma Lake

The Velma Lakes are named after the youngest daughter of Harry Oswald Constock, the manager of the Tallac House resort in the early 1900s. The approved way to reach these lakes is via the excellent trail. Following the stream up from Eagle Lake may look shorter, but one soon begins to boulder hop on rocks the size of Volkswagens and this route loses its appeal. Lower Velma Lake is less frequently visited than the other Velmas and has large specimens of the three main trout of the area. The inlet provides an area for natural reproduction. Several rock shelves provide good fly fishing points.

Middle Velma Lake

This lake is a pure rainbow fishery, and the fish achieve some size. There is no natural reproduction, due to the lack of suitable spawning areas. One can walk the shoreline and find good sized fish feeding in the shallows and off rocky points. Fly fishing is feasible from many points. There is, however, a lot of area to cover in this lake and a float tube or inflatable boat is extremely useful. Small coves may have large cruising fish. This is another lake where damselfly nymphs and adults are useful; they may be combined on a dropper with excellent effects. There are large fish here despite the pressure of humanity. This is one lake where ethics suggests catch and release of its larger specimens simply so that more anglers can enjoy them.

Upper Velma and Fontanillis Lake

Upper Velma, the smallest of the Velmas, is located on the trail up to Fontanillis Lake. There are plenty of brookies in the area and along its outlet and the lakelets downstream. One can get away from the crowds by following this stream and stalking the wily brookie (you can always pretend it's New Zealand). Fontanillis is primarily a brook trout fishery and it receives considerable pressure.

Dick's Lake

This lake and the associated Peak and Pass are named for the Hermit of Emerald Bay, Captain Richard Barter. This wild Englishman was a sailor by training and spent much of his time sailing on Tahoe. He had a tendency to partake of strong spirits while sailing and one stormy day in 1875 Barter went down with his ship. The lake which is his legacy has both brookies and rainbows and receives many visitors due to its proximity to the Pass.

Granite Lake

This small lake is the one good reason to climb the Bayview Trail. The only other possible reason to climb this dusty trail is for the view of Emerald Bay and Eagle Lake from several vantage points. The lake nonetheless has plenty of brookies, but a float tube is almost a necessity due to the overgrown nature of the shore.

One may combine a visit to this lake with a visit to Azure Lake as a strenuous but feasible day trip. One can have lunch at Azure and descend to Granite for the evening rise. It is a short jaunt back to the trailhead, but one should bring headlamps or flashlights for this adventure in case one gets carried away with the fishing and becomes "benighted."

The best fishing in this lake appears to be near the inlet stream, which is also the deepest end and farthest from the trail. Unfortunately, there are many mosquitoes in this area in early season.

Azure Lake

This gorgeous lake has gone through a number of name changes. Originally named Gladys after the daughter of Harry Oswald Constock, the name appears as Kalmeia Lake on the 1945 Forest Service map and the current Kalmia Lake was unnamed.

Following the instruction in Wood's guide it can be reached with difficulty from the Cascade Creek area or somewhat more easily from the Eagle Lake or Bayview Trail. Wood's route up Cascade Creek is often wet, requires climbing on steep and slippery rocks and is only for the very sure-footed. Though the trip up the Eagle Lake Trail is a longer distance, the high quality of the trail makes it relatively quick. I would only go up the dusty and steep Bayview Trail to Azure if I intended to stop at Granite Lake on the way back to fish the evening rise.

It is also very easy to miss the trail to Azure which, although marked on the topo, lacks a sign on the trail. This is the way to find it from the Bayview Trail: after passing the saddle between Maggie's Peaks one descends along a ridge. Soon one descends rapidly to the left (south) towards a gully but the trail turns right around a corner. That gully was the trail. Close inspection will reveal that the gully sees considerable human use. A Casio watch altimeter makes it easy to find the trail at the 8,240' level. (The Casio is a serious back country tool, the best, unless you can afford a portable Global Positioning System receiver.) If one misses this trail one soon sees the lake and is tempted to go cross-country—better to go back and find the trail than fight the bushes.

Though Azure Lake has received some rainbows, the lake itself is a solid brookie fishery with some large fish. The inlet stream provides some aerated water during the summer and is a good spot in hot weather.

Snow Lake

This lake is reached by the cross-country route up Cascade Creek. It's not hard to get lost in this area though the trail is well-ducked. The lake itself has brookies, and there are many points which give access to fly fishing. The fish in this lake appear somewhat stunted and small compared to those in Azure.

Tallac and Kalmia Lakes

Tallac is from the local Indian dialect—"tahlac" for great mountain—and this lake does live in the shadow of Mount Tallac. It has some small surviving golden plants, but is very difficult to fish due to a brushy shoreline. Access from Snow Lake should probably best be attempted with a helicopter. It is very tricky to get to Tallac from Snow Lake and the attempt should be avoided due to the steepness of the terrain. If one gets off the route the consequences could be a serious fall. The same is true for Kalmia. The route mentioned by Wood, up its outlet stream, is very dangerous due to its steepness and wetness.

Section 7: Fallen Leaf Lake

Floating Island Lake

To this day matted turf does break off and float about the lake. Unfortunately the huge cutthroat trout that once called this home are long gone. The lake is hit very hard due to its position on the main trail up Mount Tallac, but it continues to produce plenty of brookies. There are shiners in the lake and streamer patterns work well. One can fly fish with waders from the shallow shore near the trail or use roll casts in several other areas. This is a lake I would like to see restocked with the Lahontan cutthroat that originally lived here. This would provide the passerby with a little history of the area.

Cathedral Lake

When one arrives at this small tarn, one asks, "Where's the cathedral?" The cathedral is represented by the nose of Mount Tallac's southeast ridge, which appears to be a formidable mountain from the Fallen Leaf Lake region. This lakelet does contain goldens who fall for small nymph patterns. As opposed to Cup, there appear to be no scuds. They will take the blown in terrestrial and one often sees rises. The fish are usually small, and numbers vary with the success of the DFG bombing run. They do not do well if DFG hits the trees instead of the lake; this is a very small target! The lake probably represents the easiest lake with goldens to get to in the Wilderness. The fish are not big and are quick to scatter. One is rarely alone at this lake due to the traffic up Mt. Tallac and visitors spook the fish.

You can fly fish the lake from the far side as there is casting room. Alternatively, if you have waders you can fish from the near to the trail side from a shallow area. Wading, however, is a good way to spook these fish. Spin anglers are often frustrated by watching the fish follow without taking the lure. Here the smaller (and perhaps darker) the lure the better. This lake is not easy to fish, but the fish in the lake are a worthy target.

Heather Lake

This deep, wild lake is named for the low white and purple heather which border its south end. The lake is notorious for large trout. These are easier to discuss than land. The brookie population is large, and the fish are respectable with many above 12 inches. The browns are what one would like to catch here. One may find these (note: find and catch mean different things) in the boulder fields that slide into the lake from the west. Large fish often lurk along the steep drop-offs right along the trail, providing the angler with some spectacular sightseeing.

Another interesting area is the inlet, which is best reached by crossing the outlet stream (on some rotten logs) and moving along the shore towards the southwest. As one moves along this shoreline do not neglect the bays and rocky points which are much less often fished than the side of the lake on which the trail is found. There are also some rainbows in here that may use the inlet for spawning. The main reason these fish are so large is the population of redside shiners, and shiner imitations are clearly the attractor of choice. This lake can be particularly windy and is one of the few lakes where one will be thankful for having heavier equipment.

Susie Lake

This lake is either named for one of Nathan Gillmore's daughters or the matriarch of the Washoe Indians. It has a large brookie population with some fish of size. These fish will also take a fly on the surface at dawn and dusk. They are found throughout the lake, but there are good fly fishing areas on rocky points jutting into the lake at several spots.

An educational experience in this lake is to examine the inlet stream. It may run underground in dry years. This spring then becomes a major attractor for the population of brookies that are found in this lake. Other lakes have similar springs, and they are very much worth looking for.

Half Moon Lake

This lake is in a wonderful cirque with impressive views. The best campsites are along its south shore. Half Moon Lake has brookies and rainbows. I believe the rainbows spawn in the inlet stream from Alta Morris Lake. These fish, however, are hard to catch from shore due to the shallow nature of the lake shoreline. A tube is helpful to get out from the edge. If one is landlocked, one may try some of the deeper shelves that occasionally reach towards the shore.

Diversity (and frustration) can be obtained at Alta Morris Lake, which allegedly is stocked with goldens. I have yet to see a fish in this lakelet and it is small and clear enough that one can scan virtually every inch. I have had better luck finding scenery than fish at this lake.

Gilmore Lake

Nathan Gilmore first brought cattle and angora sheep to graze in the area around this lake in 1873. On the trail up from Fallen Leaf Lake one will pass through the one time resort village of Glen Alpine. The central attraction of this resort was its spring, which is well identified and the taste of which no doubt contributed to the resort's downfall.

This lake has seen stockings of virtually every species known to man, including bass. To no one's surprise brookies do the best, though recently it has received lake trout. Large browns also have been taken. This lake is over-inhabited by people, and I avoid it in full season. One of the few guides who really knows the area, Randy Johnson of Tahoma, fishes the lake successfully in early season when there are few people and the larger fish surface. With all the alternatives described above anglers can find better campsites.

The one claim to fame of this lake, which is somewhat amusing, is that it sports the only gold mine in the area. Anglers who have poor luck with the rod can try the pan at the prospect, which is located 0.25-0.50 miles directly (true) south of the south shore of the lake. There is also a very unusual and direct route leading to the lake and this area from near the end of the Lily Lake parking area. Information on this is in Wood's guide. This route is spectacular, but only for the sure-footed and those who do not suffer from acrophobia.

Grass Lake

Grass Lake is well named and located a couple of miles up the Glen Alpine Trail. It is overfished and one will have little luck with the few brookies and browns that remain hidden here.

Further Reading

Alley, Robert, *Advanced Lake Fly Fishing, The Skillful Tuber,* Frank Amato Publications, Portland, Oregon, 1991

Cole, David N., *Low-Impact Recreational Practices for Wilderness and Backcountry,* United States Department of Agriculture, Forest Service, Intermountain Research Station, Ogden, Utah 84401, (General Technical Report INT-265), 1989

Cordes, Ron and Randall Kaufmann, *Lake Fishing with A Fly,* Frank Amato Publications, Portland, Oregon, 1984

Cutter, Ralph, *Sierra Trout Guide,* Frank Amato Publications, Portland, Oregon, 1991

Forest Service, *A Guide to the Desolation Wilderness* (Forest Service Map), United States Department of Agriculture, 1990

Hill, Les and Graeme Marshall, *Stalking Trout,* Stonewall Press, Washington, D.C., 1985

Lekisch, Barbara, *Tahoe Place Names,* Great West Books, Lafayette, California, 1988

Roush, John H., *Enjoying Fishing Lake Tahoe, The Truckee River and Pyramid Lake,* Adams Press, Chicago, Illinois, 1987

Schaffer, Jeffrey P., *Desolation Wilderness and the South Lake Tahoe Basin,* Wilderness Press, Berkeley, California, 1990

Willers, Bill, *Trout Biology,* Lyons and Burford, New York, New York, 1991

Wood, Robert S., *Desolation Wilderness,* Wilderness Press, Berkeley, California, 1975

Desolation Wilderness Fishing Update
(Mail to Box 7424, Tahoe City, California 96145)

Name: _____

Address: _____

City: _____ State: _____ Zip: _____

Lake: _____ Date: _____

Number in party: _____ Total hours all members fished: _____

Species: _____ Number caught: _____ Size range: _____

Comments, amphibians seen, etc.: _____

Use reverse side or additional sheets as needed